Endorsements

"The first time I met Arjan, I knew he was a deep thinker with a unique perspective on leadership that I wanted to learn more about. As a member of his peer-mastermind group, I, along with other forerunners, have been constantly challenged to reflect on who I am from a future perspective. This pushes me to think beyond my own constraints to explore even grander outcomes than I had previously considered. His book makes it easier to review and re-engage with my ever-evolving future perspective."

—Deb Brown Maher
Perspective shifter, sales coach, business owner and author
Pennsylvania USA

"Lead the Future by Arjan Visser is not just another leadership book—it is a blueprint for transformation. Having known Arjan for nearly a decade as both a friend and trusted advisor, I have experienced firsthand the power of his insights. His coaching has helped me cultivate a future-focused mindset and align my actions with the person I see myself becoming in the future.
Thanks to Arjan's guidance, I am now consciously stepping into my future identity, embracing self-leadership with confidence and purpose. This book captures the essence of his wisdom and is an invaluable tool for anyone ready to lead with vision and authenticity."

—Pieter den Dekker
Founder of Water House Peacemaking
Organizer of the UN 2023 Water Conference
The Netherlands

LEAD THE FUTURE

“Loved reading this book—I could not put it down! It is a true toolbox for personal growth acceleration! I am so grateful to Arjan for sharing his wealth of wisdom and experience and for giving away the keys to accelerating personal growth from the inside out and reimagining the future of leadership."

—Benj Street
Accelerator of innovation and serial entrepreneur
United Kingdom

"Over the many years I have known Arjan Visser, I have consistently admired his role as both a futurist and a pioneer in spiritual leadership development.
As a business owner and network founder, Arjan’s impact on my life has been profound. His innovative coaching methods and transformative Masterminds have been invaluable to me, offering insights that have shaped my approach to leadership and strategy. His ability to connect with leaders in the present while guiding them toward the future has not only earned him global respect but has also significantly influenced my own professional journey and helped shape the direction of our global non-profit business.
Serving as a founding board member, I have witnessed firsthand how Arjan helps leaders navigate their path with clarity and purpose. Arjan is a true asset to any team he joins.
In his work, “Lead the Future” Arjan will assist you in uncovering the authentic self that the future is calling for.”

—Mark Appleyard
Co-founder of Anothen Global Ministries Inc.
North Carolina USA

“When I started Arjan's book and first glanced at the table of contents, I felt a surge of energy and excited anticipation. Knowing Arjan, I understood this would not be just another collection of ‘actionable advice,’ but something far deeper. Arjan is a true revivalist, focusing on the integration of heart, mind, and spirit to create lasting change, not just in our work but in every area of our lives. His unique ability to foresee future trends and gently guide us in adapting our vocations and workplaces accordingly is now beautifully captured in this book. I highly recommend it!”

—Laura Izard
Recruitment director at Organic Leadership
United Kingdom

"In working with Arjan, I have found clarity where there was confusion, comfort where there was pain, and insight where there was ambiguity. In this book, he has made the process more accessible than ever to prepare for tomorrow and LEAD THE FUTURE."

—Timothy Morgan
Founder of Giver Marketing Network
Oregon USA

"This book is both informative and inspirational, offering leaders at any stage the opportunity to reflect on where they are and craft new plans for making a greater impact. It is a valuable read for anyone committed to advancing their leadership journey. 100% worth it."

—Jermaine Edwards
Advisor, investor, customer growth specialist, speaker and founder of Customer Advantage and The IA Group Ltd
South Carolina USA

“Congratulations Arjan. It takes courage to put your ideas out there and I know it will be a Gamechanger for anyone who is ready to engage with the 7 steps. Having read the book and experienced you guiding me through some of the exercises, I can highly recommend this for anyone tired of the status quo but struggling on where to start developing something more inspiring and authentic. This is it. No more excuses.”

—Chris Harding
Chief game charger at Resonate Business Solution Ltd
United Kingdom

"As an entrepreneur, I am aware of the need to keep one eye firmly on the future while dealing with the needs of today. Arjan’s work as a futurist and business strategist helps me keep my future in focus and find ways to integrate the work, I am doing today to support my growth toward that future. The tools and strategies he uses allow me to think more broadly and creatively about where I am going, how to get there, and how to give more value to the people I encounter along the way."

—Shane Pope
International business director at Armatec Environmental Ltd
United Kingdom

"I met Arjan through the Giver Marketing Network and a direct introduction from Timothy Morgan. Arjan does not disappoint. When I get the chance to speak with brilliant, insightful people—especially those who are multi-lingual—I cannot help but be impressed. Beyond his insight and ability to see through the fog of surroundings, Arjan brings an authenticity to the conversation that recognizes each person’s role in the broader context of life.

When you combine faith, humility, clarity, and direction in a person's life, the result may look something like Arjan."

—Kurt Von Ahnen
Business owner of Powersports Academy and Manana No Mas, Kansas USA

"I have been working and journeying with Arjan for four years. If you want to grow in your understanding of who you are, where you want to go, and—equally importantly—where you do not want to go, then this book is for you. The 7 steps Arjan outlines are ones he has walked, is walking, and that have been the focus of our fruitful, painful, challenging, meaningful, thought-provoking, and ultimately life-giving discussions in the peer-mastermind. I warmly recommend my good friend Arjan and this book to you. In that order."

—Rob Schulz
Fellow traveler, entrepreneur, coach and investor business owner of Restoration Homes Ltd and Gladwyn Enterprise Ltd
United Kingdom

"Lead the Future" is a fascinating look into who you could become, what this might create for you, and how you can bring your future closer to today. If you invest in doing the exercises, read the book at least twice, and reach out to Arjan for guidance, I am sure you will accelerate your personal progress."

—Matt Goddard
Creator of the WORK Principle, Spiralling Upwards, and the Courageous Leaders Forum
United Kingdom

"Any amount of time spent with Arjan will leave you changed, forever. A thoughtful, charismatic, passionate, and creative individual who I am privileged to call a friend. Arjan's perspective on the future of leadership is groundbreaking, it will challenge your thinking, remove self-imposed limitations, and encourage you to look with a fresh pair of eyes on what it means to lead, and to lead in today's ever-changing world. Arjan will equip you with tools that will open new strategic channels, provide foresight and a vision of the possibilities that will radically alter the way you lead".

—Grant E Phypers
Business producer, jewellers' block
at Wilson Smith Group London Limited
United Kingdom

"Arjan has helped me, and many other leaders pursue a future that is authentic and yet beyond what we would have come up with on our own. He has a gift for asking the right questions, pressing on the right things at the right time, and facilitating people from the superficial to the supernatural.
In his book, Lead the Future, Arjan breaks down the complexities of his process into 7 easy to understand steps and provides personal applications as well. It serves as a roadmap to what can otherwise be a confusing and ambiguous process. I highly recommend Arjan's book, peer-mastermind group, and coaching to anyone who wants to pursue a more meaningful future and elevate their leadership impact!"

—Ryan Rigterink
Founder of Workgaze and author of *Redesign Life: Finding Purpose and Balance Amidst Chaos and Uncertainty*
Michigan USA

“This book deserves a sequel. Arjan is not focused on playing down the old or fixing what already exists. He is all about the future—the future you. It is not about past results, but about uncovering your unique, added value.
The book is so practical and impactful that I am eager to hear the testimonies of the forerunners who contributed to this incredible manual, as well as those that will emerge from it. If you get the chance, do not miss the opportunity to have Arjan as one of your peers.”

—David Koerts
Visionary catalyst, entrepreneur, investor
and business owner at In2Purpose B.V
The Netherlands

"I think a lot about creating a 400-year impact, and I do not know many coaches or thinkers whose idea of creating a better future really goes beyond a three-year plan... but Arjan Visser routinely astonishes me with his ability to bring a twist in the conversation, helping me think differently about how to envision and create a better future that lasts. In his book, Lead the Future, he unlocks timeless insights that feel like secrets yet are accessible to anyone willing to engage. Get the book and dive in."

—Adam G. Fleming
ICF Professional Certified Coach
Co-author of *The Legacy Way: Walking into Purpose*
Indiana USA

“So simple in its approach, yet “Lead the Future” holds a depth that will require multiple readings to fully absorb its insights, allowing them to sink into both mind and heart. Each reading brings new layers of understanding, helping me think more deeply about who I can become.

But why go through it alone? By joining the peer-mastermind group, I can accelerate my journey into the future, receiving real-time feedback and support from Arjan and fellow forerunners. The impact of his book and mastermind has the potential to transform not only how I see myself, but how I step into the future. I know which option I will choose…"

—Jon Mullen
Business imagineer and owner of Clearly Net Zero
United Kingdom

"I have come to know Arjan as an inspiring and visionary leader who has consistently challenged and guided me in shaping my future identity. His approach has sparked groundbreaking insights and led to pivotal personal choices in my life. Arjan has played a significant role in the profound transformation I have undergone, both in my career and personally, and I am immensely grateful to him and his peer community for their contributions.

His book, Lead the Future, outlines the different phases of his approach and is filled with thought-provoking questions that encourage you to think bigger than you ever thought possible. Arjan inspires and guides you to take the next step in self-leadership and personal development, helping you to discover your purpose and bring real meaning to it as you move toward your future."

—Raymond Leenders
Interim people leader and strategic creative facilitator
Business owner at Leaders in Nature
The Netherlands

"Over the decades, I have met many coaches, gurus, and thought leaders, but none quite like Arjan Visser. His depth and breadth of understanding of people, human institutions, and their relationships is rare. He caringly shares this understanding in sensible, easily consumed ways for the benefit of others. Arjan uses it to challenge people to grow, both personally and within their institutions. And he does so, not from a lofty or abstract place, but like a wise friend across the coffee table. Listen to him."

—Joe Chiarella
Strategic Thinking, Foresight, and Guidance
Florida USA

7-Steps to Expand Your Identity, Strategic Foresight, and Vision

ARJAN VISSER

LEAD THE FUTURE

7 STEPS

To Expand Your Identity,
Strategic Foresight,
and Vision

ARJAN VISSER

Publisher: SCAP Books, a SCAP Management B.V. company
E-mail Address: books@scapmanagement.com
Book ISBN: 978-90-834756-1-5
Hardcover ISBN: 978-90-834756-7-7
eBook ISBN: 978-90-834756-0-8

Printed on-demand

Contents

"To the forerunners who exemplify true leadership—bringing forth, going ahead, clearing the path—and who lead the future as a horizon of endless possibilities, ready to create, grow, and step into who they are becoming."

7-Steps to Expand Your Identity, Strategic Foresight, and Vision

ARJAN VISSER

Acknowledgments

So many people have contributed to and inspired me over the years to write this book, and I want to express my deepest gratitude.

To my soulmate, Sascha—my travel companion in life, business, and society. You travel the future with me daily, and I love you. You reminded me to push further, aim higher, and lead from within, even when circumstances scream otherwise. You made this journey possible, and I owe it to you to finish well.

To my world changers, Floris (my brightness), Maurits (my rest), and Pepijn (my adventure)—I cannot wait to see you lead in life, business, and society. You inspire me, and you are the future.

Thank you, Mom and Dad, Bram and Ria, for teaching me to make choices and take a stand for what is right, even when it means going against the flow. You laid the foundation from which I now lead the future.

David Martin, your wise counsel helped me embrace being wired differently and explore what that truth holds. Mark Appleyard, your wisdom has always guided me forward when I lost my way. Benj Street, your unlimited encouragement and belief in me kept me accelerating. Pieter den Dekker, your pivotal interventions and reflections made the difference—your steadfast friendship has deeply influenced my journey.

To my dear friends who shaped this manuscript—Deb Brown Maher, your divine wisdom brought clarity when I needed it most; Ryan Rigterink, our deep conversations refined my voice; and Chris Harding, you always pushed the boundaries of my understanding.

Finally, to all my peers, friends, and clients—especially Rob Schulz, Shane Pope, Laura Izard, Grant Phypers, Matt Goddard, Jon Mullen, Ivonne Verkes, and David Koerts—thank you for shaping the language and message of this book. Your impact is immeasurable, and I honor each of you.

Invitation by the Author

I am Arjan Visser, a friend and sparring partner to decision-makers who are ready to elevate their leadership. Over the years, I have had the privilege of working closely with leaders who possess the courage to proactively explore their full potential and make impactful choices. It is from these experiences that this book was born. *LEAD THE FUTURE: 7 Steps to Expand Your Identity, Strategic Foresight and Vision* is an invitation to go beyond what you already know and to step up in leadership—not just for your organization, but for yourself. I believe that everyone is born with the gift of leadership, which is a responsibility that requires intention and effort to bring to maturity. The choices you and I make, or the ones we avoid, ripple through our lives and the lives of those around us, leaving an imprint that echoes far beyond the present moment.

My main objective with this book is to inspire you to embrace self-leadership from the inside out. The 7 steps you are about to explore are not just a manual—they are a learning tool designed to ignite your journey towards mature, authentic and healthy leadership. I know that prioritizing self-development can feel daunting, especially when there are so many other demands on your time. But I challenge you to consider: What could happen if you increased your influence as a leader? What might you see if you could positively impact those around you with a new level of intensity? This book will guide you through the journey of taking charge of your self-leadership, surrounding yourself with the right peers, and aligning your daily actions with your long-term vision.

This book is not intended to optimize anyone's comfort zone. It is grounded in my own experiences of developing and nurturing a future mindset over the past decade. For me, a future mindset means pursuing, with purpose and passion, an understanding of who you can become. It goes beyond just forward looking and thinking about the future. It is about stepping up with purpose, finding your voice, aligning your business with your future perspective, inspiring those around you and serving your clients with the value you create.

So, I invite you to start this journey with an open mind and a willing heart. The path to authentic and healthy leadership is not easy in any way, but it is profoundly rewarding. Let this book be your guide as you step into your future self and lead with the authenticity and vision that the world is waiting for.

August 20th, 2024

Arjan Visser

Introduction

The Leader's Journey to Lead the Future

Leadership is an inside-out journey, not just a set of skills to be mastered. In a world that is constantly evolving, the most successful leaders are those who are dedicated to creating the future rather than merely managing reactions. If this resonates with you, then this book is your guide to becoming that kind of leader—one who not only envisions the future but actively shapes it.

The journey you are invited to embark upon is both introspective and forward-looking. Each chapter is designed to help you expand your identity, develop strategic foresight, and refine your vision for the future. You will learn how to envision your future self, broaden your perspective, embrace your emerging authority, build a supportive network, engage in peer development, strengthen your voice, and align your business strategies with your personal discoveries. These seven steps are not just about enhancing your leadership skills; they are about transforming you into a leader who leads with authenticity, clarity, and purpose.

Why Personal Development is Crucial for Healthy Leadership?

At the core of healthy leadership is a commitment to ongoing personal development. Leadership is not just about managing people and situations; it is about understanding and leading yourself first. Your ability to lead others effectively is directly tied to your level of self-awareness and your dedication to personal growth. As you continue to grow and evolve, so too does your capacity to lead. This is why personal development is not just important—it is crucial for healthy, effective and visionary leadership.

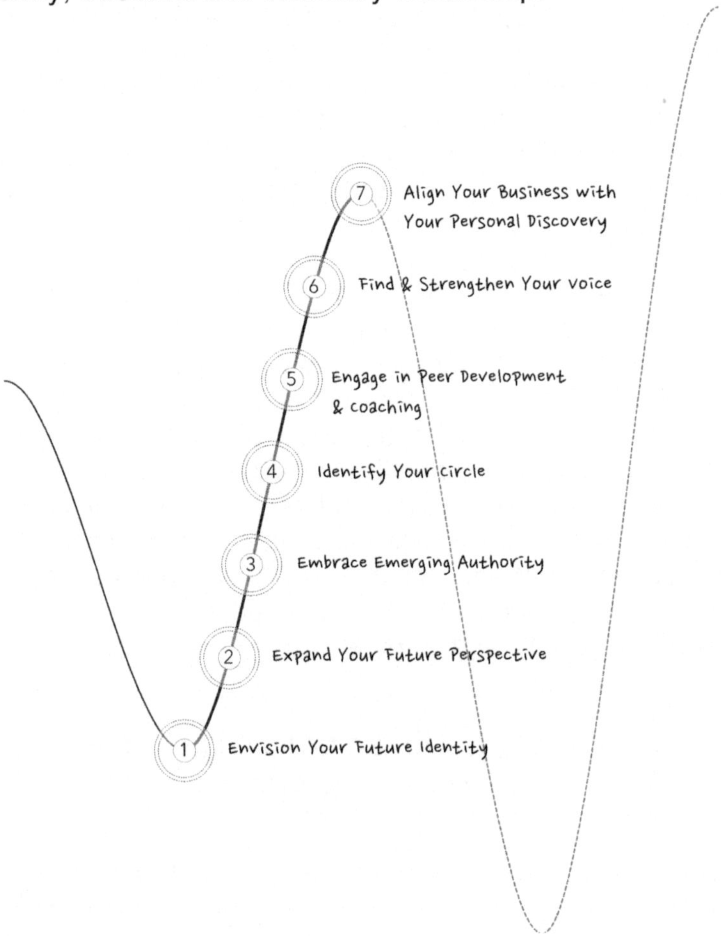

This illustration shows how to position the 7 steps on a self-development tool, such as Theory U, extended with the perspective of seeing life as a rhythm. It represents a circular development process over time, with an increasing flow of influence, impact, and authority.

In this book, each of the seven steps is designed to guide you through a process of self-discovery and expansion of your consciousness - i.e. seeing more of what is really in play and what is possible. From defining your future identity to aligning your business strategies with your personal discoveries, these steps will help you build a solid foundation for leading the future.

The key question here is: Why is personal development crucial for advancing and sustaining your leadership journey? The answer lies in the understanding that to lead others into the future, you must first lead yourself.

How to Use This Guide

This guide is designed to be informative, reflective and actionable. It is not just about reading; it is about engaging deeply with the concepts and practices presented in each chapter. As you move through the book, you will be encouraged to reflect on your own experiences, use your imagination, challenge your assumptions, and take concrete steps toward becoming the leader you aspire to be.

A proven approach to activate your imagination and forward-looking skills is to combine creative thinking tools and hands-on learning experience methods. It is a way to step aside from rational thinking.
If you can, grab a random set of LEGO® bricks to help you build and visualize answers you have not seen before and then verbalize the meaning of the elements that you build to create new language. From these further new insights, you are then able to define actions. Summarized, it is a process of Revelation, Interpretation and Application, aka R.I.A.

The outcome of this process is a deeper understanding of yourself as a leader and a stronger connection between your personal growth and professional responsibilities. By committing to actively engage with all seven steps, you will equip yourself with the tools and insights needed to stay relevant and effective in a rapidly changing world.

Take a moment to reflect on your recent personal and professional growth experiences.

- When have you felt most aligned with your authentic self in your leadership roles?
- What moments of foresight or hindsight stand out to you as pivotal?
- What do the three dimensions of the book (expand my identity, strategic foresight and vision) mean to you?

Use these reflections to write down an intention for how you will approach the learning process in this guide. This is not just a book—it is a roadmap for your future.

Write Down Your Reflection.
What is your approach to expanding your identity, to sharpen your strategic foresight and deepening your vision?

My intentions for expanding my identity, strategic foresight and vision are:

By the end of this journey, you will have not only expanded your identity and vision but also strengthened your ability to lead with authenticity and foresight. The tangible fruit of your commitment will be a sustainable leadership approach that balances personal growth with professional impact. Welcome to the beginning of your transformative journey to *Lead the Future.*

Step 1

Envision Your Future Identity

In a rapidly changing world, the most successful leaders are those who not only navigate the present moment but also envision a compelling future for themselves. To lead most effectively into the future, it is essential to have a clear understanding of who you aspire to become. Your future identity is not just a distant dream or a role to play; it is a guiding force that shapes your decisions and actions today. By defining and embracing a fuller version of yourself, you align your leadership with your deepest values, beliefs, and intrinsic motivations, setting the stage for sustained growth and impact.

Let's begin the process of envisioning your future identity—an identity that not only reflects your current aspirations but also aligns with the long-term outcomes you seek to achieve. By the end, you will have a powerful tool—a personal "I am" statement—that will serve as a constant reminder of the leader you are becoming.

Defining The Fuller Version of Your Identity

To lead with purpose and clarity, you must first have a clear vision of your future self. True leadership begins with a deep understanding of who you are at your core, and who you are called to become.

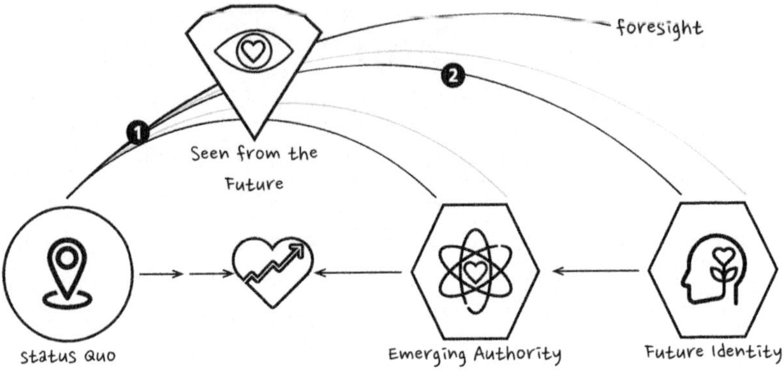

This illustration provides an overview of the futurizing process to envision the fuller version of your identity (your unknown self) in two steps. Step 1 involves shifting your perspective to perceive today's reality and the near future as if you are viewing it from a future vantage point. Step 2 focuses on using your imagination to explore this vantage point and find language to express who you can become. As you progress, this approach leads to your emerging authority and strategies, enabling you to shape and lead the future.

This vision of your future identity is not about employment-based titles or achievements; it is about connecting with the essence of who you are and who you aspire to be. By defining a fuller, more authentic version of your identity, you ensure that your leadership is grounded in what truly matters to you. This process involves uncovering your core values, the beliefs that drive you, and the intrinsic motivations that propel you forward. It is about asking yourself, "What does the fullest version of my future identity look like? Who can I become?" and allowing the answer to shape the way you lead today.

This clarity will serve as your compass, guiding your decisions and actions towards a future that resonates with your true self.

Crafting Your Future Identity "I am" Statement

Once you have a vision of your future identity, the next step is to articulate it clearly and powerfully. This is where the "I am" statement comes in—a succinct declaration of who you are becoming. This statement is not just a motivational phrase; it is a personal leadership declaration that embodies the characteristics, attributes, and values of your future self.

To craft your "I am" statement, engage in deep self-reflection. Visualize your ideal future self and verbalize the qualities that define you in that vision. What strengths do you embody? What impact do you have? How do you lead? Record and transcribe these reflections into a cohesive statement that resonates with your identity and aspirations.

This "I am" statement is a tangible fruit of your introspection, serving as a daily guide and reminder of the leader you are evolving into. Revisit it daily, speak it out loud, and let it anchor your leadership journey.

Craft Your Future Identity Statement.
Take the vantage point of who you will have become in the next 12 months? Start your statement with I am.

Imagine stepping into a time machine like the one from the *Back to the Future* movies. You travel 12 months into the future and pick up the leading magazine in your field. It is the issue dated 12 months from now, and your photo is on the cover. You have made it to the cover due to an incredible year full of breakthroughs, achievements, and recognized influence. In the interview for the article, you introduce yourself with your new "I am statement". This statement reflects your future identity—Who you will have become in the next 12 months.

I am

I am (second iteration)

You can iterate as much as needed to capture a clear and inspiring "I am" statement that reflects the fuller version of your future identity. This statement is more than words—it is a powerful tool that will guide you as you navigate your leadership journey, helping you to stay aligned with your core values and long-term vision. As you move forward, your "I am" statement will serve as a beacon, illuminating the path to the leader you are destined to become.

Step 2

Expand Your Future Perspective

To lead with vision is to see beyond the present moment and anticipate the opportunities and challenges that lie ahead. Expanding your future perspective is not just about predicting trends or reacting to change—it is about actively shaping the future you sense and want to create. As a leader, your ability to envision a compelling and expansive future is crucial for strategic decision-making and long-term success. In this step, you will begin to imagine your preferred future, helping you to align your actions today with the future you desire to build.

By broadening your perspective and grounding it in your core values and identity, you can create a roadmap that not only leads to personal and professional fulfillment but also positions you as a visionary leader. This exercise in forward-looking will enable you to anticipate future needs and opportunities, ensuring that your leadership remains relevant and impactful.

Understanding Your Preferred Future

A leader's vision is the cornerstone of strategic decision-making and long-term success. Understanding your preferred future starts with a creative and imaginative journey, taking you beyond your current horizon. It involves asking yourself, "What does my preferred future look like?" and allowing yourself to dream beyond the constraints of the present moment. This process is more than wishful thinking—it is a deliberate exercise in shaping a future that aligns with your future identity and values.

To truly grasp your preferred future, you must engage in deep reflection on your aspirations and the legacy you wish to leave. Consider the impact you want your work to have, the growth you wish to see and home and the influence you want to have in your society. This clarity will help you to make decisions today that are aligned with your long-term vision. By envisioning your future with intentionality, you lay the groundwork for the strategic foresight that will guide your leadership journey.

Describe Your Preferred Future.
Take the view at the edge of your horizon and envisioning the areas of life, at home, at work and in society.

Close your eyes and imagine you are on a beach, watching enormous waves. As you look at yourself, you see that you are fully equipped to ride the waves. You even have the courage to take on the challenge. With a bit of practice, you are able to ride the highest wave of them all. Your view of the horizon is breathtaking and incredibly detailed—you can even see beyond it, envisioning your future in all areas of life, at home, at work, and in society. Verbalize, record, and transcribe what you see in detail.

My preferred future look like:

Creating Your Future Timeline

With a clear vision of your preferred future, the next step is to map out the journey toward it. Creating a future timeline allows you to chart a course that aligns with your long-term vision, breaking it down into actionable steps and learning milestones. This timeline is not just a series of dates—it is a dynamic plan that reflects both your personal and professional aspirations, helping you to stay on track and make informed decisions.

Begin by identifying learning milestones that mark significant progress toward your ideal future. These could include career achievements, personal growth goals, or pivotal moments in your leadership journey. Once your timeline is established, focus on the present moment: identify one key decision you can make today that moves you closer to reaching your first learning milestones towards your future vision. This proactive approach ensures that your daily actions are aligned with your long-term goals, making your preferred future a reality.

Fill in Your Learning Milestones and Daily Actions. Focus on what you want to learn in the next year. Divide them into 90-day periods and decide what daily actions you can add to your daily routines to pursue learning.

Choose your learning milestones based on the future areas where you anticipate future progress. Think in terms of a one-year timeline, divided into 90-day periods. Focus on what you want to learn and resist the temptation to predict specific results. This approach will help you discover future outcomes and prevent you from repeating past patterns driven by your understanding of the past, rather than making your preferred future a reality.

Step 2: Expand Your Future Perspective

	Learning Milestones	Daily Actions
Next 90 days		
+ 90 days		
+ 90 days		
+ 90 days		

You have taken the first step in developing a future timeline—a high level but actionable roadmap to your long-term vision. With your timeline, you are ready to make decisions today that align with your future perspective, leading with purpose and direction into the future.

Step 3

Embrace Emerging Authority

As you expand your future identity and perspective, your authority as a leader will naturally begin to emerge. This authority is not about titles or positions; it is about the unique value and perspective you bring to your "metron," sphere of influence, impact and authority. Embracing this emerging authority means stepping confidently into the role that your future identity and perspective demand. It is about recognizing that your voice matters and that your unique message has the power to influence and inspire others.

This step will guide you through the process of developing and sharing your unique message—one that is authentically aligned with your future identity and value promise for those around you. By the end of this step, you will have the tools to establish yourself as a thought leader in your field, capable of guiding others toward a shared vision of the future.

Developing Your Unique Message

Authentic authority is rooted in the clarity and power of your unique message. This message reveals the authority gained by overcoming a "mess" in your life. It reflects your core values, beliefs, and the promise you make to those you lead. It is the essence of what you stand for and the value you promise within your "metron".

To develop this message, you must first understand what sets you apart—what unique perspective or value promise do you bring to your sphere of influence?

Your authority emerges when you align this message with your future identity. This alignment not only strengthens your leadership but also ensures that your influence resonates deeply with those who need it most. The objective here is to craft a message that feels authentic, speaks directly to your audience, and positions you as a trusted voice in your field. By articulating your unique message, you begin to establish the foundation for thought leadership, guiding others with your vision and insight.

Building Thought Leadership in Your Metron

With a clear and compelling message, the next step is to build thought leadership within your "metron". Thought leadership is about more than just expertise; it is about leading conversations, influencing perspectives, and shaping the future of your sphere of influence, industry or community. To do this effectively, you must first understand the "fix" you are offering—what problems do you solve, and what future do you help create when you step up?

Start by writing a personal manifesto that outlines your leadership promises and principles you stand by. This manifesto will serve as a guiding document, helping you to remain focused on your core message as you begin to share it more widely. Once your message is refined, start sharing it among peers who do not share a stake in your success. This allows you to fine-tune your message before engaging in broader speaking engagements, writing, or social media. As you consistently share your message, your authority will grow, and you will establish yourself as a thought leader in your “metron”.

Write Your Personal Manifesto

Start by reflecting on the impact of your presence: what problems are solved and what future becomes accessible when you step up? This deep reflection will help you uncover your core beliefs about yourself.

Promise 1. What 'fix' am I carrying now that becomes available when I show up?

Promise 2. What 'future' is being created and becomes accessible when I step up?

Be mindful to find your 3 principles, which nurture your value promises. These are principles you have learned through overcoming challenges. Identify the principles you (sub-)consciously choose to live by, to inspire others and nurture your promises.

Principle 1. What have I learned and what do I live by to nurture my promise(s)?

Principle 2. What have I learned and what do I live by to nurture my promise(s)?

Principle 3. What have I learned and what do I live by to nurture my promise(s)?

Embracing your emerging authority is an iterative process, requiring your dedication to pursue and persevere. As you step into your emerging authority, you are not only shaping your own future but also influencing the future of those around you. The outcome of this chapter depends on your deep reflection on the core of your unique message, which sets you apart and positions you as a thought leader. This core will guide you as you navigate your leadership journey, helping you inspire and lead others with confidence and clarity. With your unique value promise and perspective, you are well-equipped to *Lead the Future* with authority and vision.

Step 4

Identify Your Circle

As you expand your future identity and embrace your emerging authority, the relationships you cultivate become increasingly vital to your growth and acceleration. The circle of people you surround yourself with—peers, clients, and mentors—will either accelerate you toward your future vision or hold you back. Identifying and strategically building this circle is essential for aligning your personal and professional life with your long-term goals.

In this step, you will learn how to map out your current network and intentionally cultivate relationships that support your evolving future identity and perspective. By choosing your circle wisely, you create a powerful support system that not only reflects your true self but also accelerates your journey toward future success.

Mapping Your Network for Tomorrow

The people you surround yourself with have a profound impact on your growth as a leader. Your network should not just reflect your current state but should also be aligned with the future you envision for yourself. This means being intentional about the relationships you cultivate—ensuring they support your future identity and emerging authority.

To begin, take stock of your current network. Who are the individuals that consistently challenge you to grow, who provide wisdom and perspective, and who align with your long-term vision?

Mapping out your network for tomorrow involves identifying those key relationships that will be instrumental in helping you achieve your goals. This exercise will guide you in building a circle that nurtures your aspirations and drives you toward your future. By understanding who is in your corner and who may need to be added, you lay the groundwork for a network that will support your continued development.

Strategically Choosing Peers, Clients, and Mentors

Once you have a clear understanding of your current network, the next step is to strategically choose the peers, clients, and mentors who will support your future vision. Each relationship you cultivate should serve a purpose—whether it is to challenge your thinking, provide guidance, or open new opportunities. The goal is to build a network that is both diverse and aligned with your personal and professional aspirations.

Start by identifying the key relationships that are already in your life and assess how they contribute to your growth. Then, map out any gaps in your network—areas where you need more support or different perspectives. Once these gaps are identified, take proactive steps to fill them. This might involve reaching out to a potential mentor who embodies the qualities you aspire to or connecting with a peer who shares your vision for the future. By doing so, you create a network that not only reflects where you are but also where you are going.

Map Your Network for the Future
Who accelerates your growth or holds you back? Which relationships are vital for your future to be cultivated, and which ones do you have to let go?

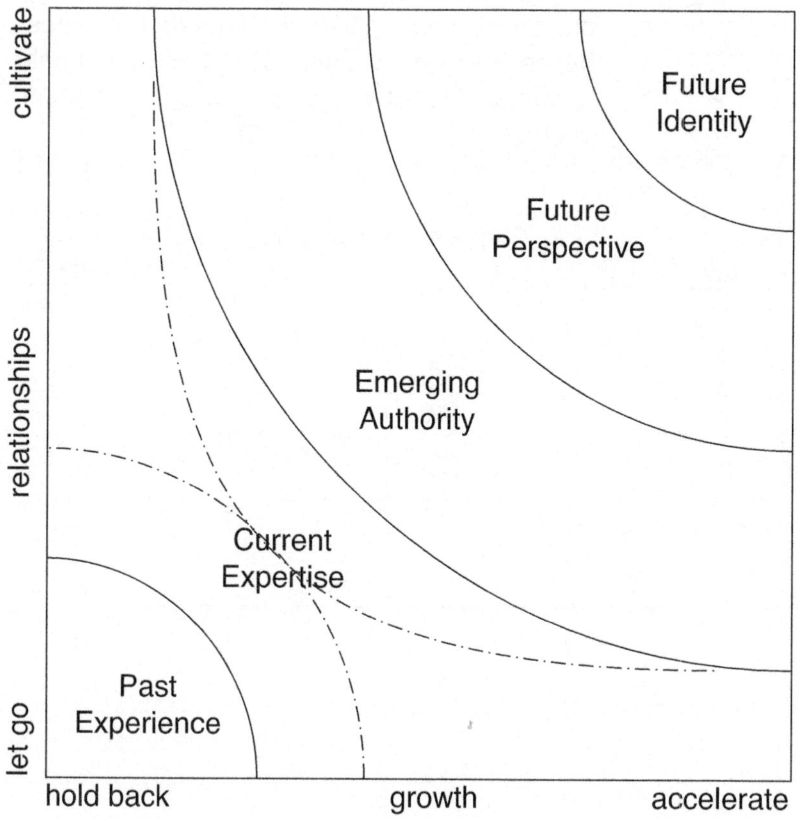

Choose your relationships strategically
Which five key relationships do you need to nurture and measure progress?

Choose up to five key relationships that support your growth and help accelerate the realization of your preferred future. Be thoughtful about the (shared) purpose of each relationship, how you can nurture it to maintain its purpose, and the outcomes you anticipate. Measure progress based on these outcomes and continually redefine the purpose and nurturing as needed over time.

Key Relationship	Purpose	Nurturing	Anticipated Outcome

By highlighting the key relationships that will support your future growth, you will have a clear and actionable map of your network. This network will be a crucial asset as you continue to expand your identity, strategic foresight, and vision. With a thoughtfully chosen circle around you, you are better equipped to navigate the challenges of leadership and achieve the long-term outcomes you aspire to. Your network becomes a reflection of your journey—a powerful force that accelerates you toward your future self.

Step 5

Engage in Peer Development & Coaching

As you continue your journey to expand your identity, strategic foresight, and vision, the role of peer development and coaching becomes increasingly important. These tools provide the support, feedback, and accountability needed to refine your leadership skills and ensure that you stay aligned with your long-term goals. Engaging with peers and coaches who are on a similar path can lead to breakthroughs in self-awareness and growth, helping you navigate the complexities of leadership with greater confidence and clarity.

This step explores the transformative power of peer learning and coaching, offering insights into how these practices can elevate your leadership. By the end of this chapter, you will be equipped to seek out and engage in peer-masterminds and coaching programs that foster continual growth and development.

The Power of Peer Learning and Coaching

One of the most effective ways to accelerate your leadership development is through learning with and from others who are on a similar journey. Peer learning and coaching offer unique opportunities for growth that are difficult to achieve alone.

These practices enable you to gain new perspectives, challenge your assumptions, and receive constructive feedback from individuals who understand the challenges you face.

The core concept here is that leadership is not a solitary endeavor. By actively participating in peer development and coaching, you tap into a collective wisdom that can enhance your decision-making, deepen your self-awareness, and sharpen your strategic foresight. This collaborative approach fosters a sense of (self-) accountability and (intrinsic) motivation, helping you to stay on track with your personal and professional goals. The objective is to encourage you to embrace these powerful tools for continual growth, recognizing that the journey is much richer when shared with others

Joining Peer-Masterminds and Coaching Programs

To fully experience the benefits of peer learning and coaching, it is essential to take concrete steps to prepare yourself to join these types of programs. Peer-masterminds, in particular, offer a structured environment where leaders can come together to share experiences, solve problems, and support each other's growth. Similarly, coaching programs provide personalized guidance that is tailored to your specific needs and challenges, helping you to unlock your potential and achieve your long-term vision.

By joining a peer-mastermind group or a coaching program, you immerse yourself in a community of like-minded leaders who are committed to growth and development. The outcome is a deeper understanding of your leadership strengths and areas for improvement, as well as increased accountability to your goals. The tangible fruit of this engagement is not just insight, but a network of supportive relationships that accelerate you forward. To start, seek out or join a peer-mastermind group that aligns with your leadership development goals, and commit to regular participation in a coaching program that challenges you to grow.

Are You Ready to Join a Peer-Mastermind Group? Use the 7 P's to Guide Your Decision:

	I Want	Not Now
1. Priority: *Are you dedicated to prioritizing your personal growth and self-development, as essential to your leadership journey?*		
2. Perceive: *Are you ready to recognize and harness greater influence, understanding how it could transform your leadership?*		
3. Position: *Are you prepared to take intentional action to develop and refine your leadership approach?*		
4. Permission: *Are you prepared to give and receive honest feedback that drives growth and improvement?*		
5. Perspective: *Are you open to embrace a forward-thinking mindset and explore new ideas and possibilities, even in the face of uncertainty?*		

6. Preference: *Are you willing to engage with peers who will support and challenge you, knowing that this discomfort is where true growth happens?*		
7. Pursue: *Are you committed to aligning your actions with your long-term vision and investing fully in your leadership development?*		

By reflecting on these 7 P's, you can determine if you want to join a peer-mastermind group and take your leadership to the next level.

Engaging in peer development and coaching is a crucial step in expanding your identity, strategic foresight, and vision. Through these practices, you gain the insight, accountability, and support needed to navigate the challenges of leadership with greater clarity and confidence. The outcome is a stronger, more resilient leader who is equipped to *Lead the Future* with vision and purpose. As you continue to invest in your growth through peer-masterminds and coaching, you build a foundation of continual development that will serve you throughout your leadership journey.

Step 6

Find & Strengthen Your Voice

As a leader, your voice is one of your most powerful tools. It is the medium through which your vision, values, and identity are communicated to the world. Finding and strengthening your voice is not just about speaking up—it is about aligning your message with your future identity and using it to inspire and influence those around you. The journey to discovering your authentic voice requires exploration, experimentation, and refinement. By strengthening your voice, you not only clarify your own leadership path but also become a beacon for others, guiding them toward a shared future vision.

In this step, we will explore how to find new language that accurately reflects your future perspective and how to share that voice effectively to shape the future you wish to create. The goal is to help you refine your communication so that it resonates deeply with your audience and amplifies your impact as a leader.

Finding New Language to Express Your Perspective

Your leadership voice is a direct expression of your future identity. As you evolve, so should the language you use to communicate your strategic foresight and vision.

This process involves more than just choosing the right words; it is about finding new language that authentically reflects your journey and resonates with those you seek to influence. A strong, clear voice is crucial for leadership because it is through this voice that you will inspire action, foster alignment, and lead change.
The objective here is to help you discover new ways to articulate your evolving future identity and perspective. This requires both introspection and experimentation. As you refine your voice, consider how it aligns with your long-term goals and how it can be a tool to increase your influence within your "metron", or even extend it, whether that is your industry, community, or sphere of influence. The key question to guide this exploration is: How can you refine and amplify your voice to better resonate with others and increase your influence?

A proven method for this is the 60-second micro-pitch and 15-minute micro-talk exercises used in the Business Revivalists' peer-mastermind group.

Craft Your 60-second Micro-Pitch
Find new language to articulate your future identity (your unknown self).

Create your 'pitch' for an audience who need:
1. to 'hear' your 'authentic' future identity*.
2. to 'taste' what you are about.
3. to 'see' the right facet of you.
4. to 'smell' you are genuine*.
5. to 'feel' you are in the lead till the end!
*review your notes from step 1, 2 and 3.

1. **Introduce who you will have become in the next 12 months:**

I am ..

2. **Be purposeful about your experiences and intrinsic motivation:**

3. **Resonate and connect with the listener's need:**

4. **Be meaningful about where you go to and promise your value:**

5. **Invite for 'an espresso', swap contact details, ask for help or agree on the next steps:**

Write Your 15-Minute Micro-Talk

Find new language to articulate your emerging authority and your voice.

Write your 'talk' for an audience who need you:
1. to be vulnerable and authentic to create trust.
2. to model life, leading and learning*.
3. to share your value promises*.
4. to inspire to take ownership.
5. to stay in the lead till the end!

*review your notes from step 1, 2 and 3

1. **Connect - help your audience to connect with your heart:**

Be careful not to create a victim/ villain tension with your story

2. **Message - what 'mess' have you overcome and what principles did you learn?**

3. **Testimony – what have you 'tested well' and can promise your audience and yourself?**

4. **Move to Action – how will you exercise your authority and prompt others to engage with you?**

5. **Empower – give your audience hope. Help them to believe it is possible and accessible for them to be victorious too:**

Sharing Your Voice to Create the Future

Once you have found new language, the next step is to share your voice. The way you communicate your future perspective and identity can either rally others to your cause or leave your message unheard. To create the future you envision, your voice needs to be clear, compelling, and consistent. It is not just about speaking; it is about making your voice a driving force that shapes the trajectory of your leadership and the broader future.

The outcome of this process is a refined communication style that not only articulates your future identity and emerging authority but also inspires others to follow your lead. The tangible fruit is a leadership voice that resonates with your target audience, making your vision a shared one. To achieve this, practice articulating your unique voice and perspective in a concise, impactful manner. Start by delivering and fine-tuning a speech in a safe environment, such as a peer-mastermind group that does not have a stake in your progress. This allows you to receive honest and constructive feedback and discover how your voice resonates before taking it public.

Finding and strengthening your voice is a dynamic process that directly impacts your ability to *Lead the Future.* By refining your language and sharing your perspective with confidence, you ensure that your leadership voice is not only heard but also embraced. The outcome is a powerful, authentic voice that clearly communicates your vision and inspires others to join you on the journey. As you continue to practice and refine your voice, you will find that it becomes a vital tool in shaping the future you wish to create.

Step 7

Align Your Business with Your Personal Discovery

This step focuses on leaders who are in a position to explore how to integrate their personal insights with or and their business strategies, leading to greater fulfillment and success.

As a leader, your personal growth and professional strategies should not exist in separate spheres. The insights you gain from self-discovery and the evolution of your future identity are powerful catalysts for transforming your business or career. Aligning your business with your personal discovery ensures that your work remains meaningful, sustainable, and in harmony with your long-term vision.

The objective of this chapter is to help you bring your evolving future identity into alignment with your business strategies. By doing so, you will ensure that your professional path reflects who you are becoming and the future you envision. This alignment is crucial for creating a business that not only thrives but also remains deeply connected to your authority and aspirations.

Realigning Business Strategies with Your Future Perspective

Your business strategies should evolve as you do. As you gain clarity on your future identity and long-term vision, it is essential to realign your professional strategies to reflect these changes. This alignment creates coherence between who you are, what you value, and how you lead your business. It also ensures that your business is not just a vehicle for profit but a true reflection of your identity and authority.

The core concept here is that business strategies must be dynamic, continually adapting to reflect personal growth and the foresight you have developed. The objective is to guide you in evaluating your current strategies and making necessary adjustments to ensure they align with your evolving future identity and perspective. The key question to consider is: How can you adjust your business strategies to better reflect your evolving future identity, foresight, and vision?

Conducting a Strategic Rhythms Review

To maintain alignment between your personal growth and business objectives, it is important to regularly review your strategic rhythms. Strategic rhythms are the recurring processes that keep your business on track, such as strategic design cycles, performance reviews, and innovation sessions. Conducting a Strategic Rhythms Review ensures that these processes are aligned with your future perspective and personal development.

The outcome of this review is the indicator for an iteration of your business strategy that is not only aligned with your personal growth but also equipped to adapt to emerging opportunities and challenges. The tangible outcome is a new strategy that reflects your future identity and perspective, making your business a powerful expression of who you are. To achieve this, review your current strategic rhythms and identify areas that need realignment. Consider initiating annual strategic rhythms to ensure your business stays in sync with your evolving foresight and vision, creating a future that is both intentional and inspiring.

Strategic Rhythm Review:

A workable future vision outlines the next "summit" on the horizon. With a 3-to-5-year horizon, you can encompass the relational context of yourself, your team, your organization, your clients, and your society. This is your playing field for shared purpose and relational goals, enabling you to create specific narratives to communicate your worldview effectively.

3–to-5-year Common Vision	Yes	Not Yet
Common Vision: *Has your organization-wide vision been updated in the last 3 years?*		
Annual Reflection: *Does your visioning process include annual reflections that allow for fine-tuning based on your evolving future identity and perspective?*		

A Strategic Design addresses the strategic paradoxes faced by each business (unit). These resolved paradoxes represent the complexity and tension between present challenges and future opportunities. To carefully balance and navigate the right path to the envisioned vision “summit”. A typical time span is 12 months for a Strategic Design

Strategic Paradox (annual)	Yes	Not Yet
Future Perspective: *Are your preferred future, winning aspirations, and future goals clearly (re-) defined and aligned with your evolving future identity and perspective?*		
Present Challenge: *Have you clearly (re-) identified which customer jobs are accomplished by acquiring your products, services, or engagement, and understood the needs, wants, expectations, or styles involved with their current obstacles or future desires?*		

Great Choices: *Have you (re-) defined a great resolution that serves your customer and creates a better future for both of you.*		

A Strategic Design addresses your unique value promise and client relationships by specifically addressing clients who resonate with your future perspective.
It focuses on the challenge to serving their current needs, wants, styles, and expectations, while also ensuring that they become integral to your future success.

Strategic Challenge (annual)	Yes	Not Yet
Unique Value Promise: *Have you (re-)defined the unique value you promise your customer that addresses their wants and creates a sustainable competitive advantage for their future?*		
Client Engagement: *Have you (re-)identified the engagement that provides the best experience to extend and expand your relationship with your client?*		
Future Growth: *Have you (re-)identified the success factors you need to measure to stay focused on people, planet, and profit to achieve a breakthrough?*		

A Strategic Design formulates a strategy map to navigate the business (unit) toward its next "basecamp" and, ultimately, to the vision summit. Over a 12-month period, typically three strategic maps are required to progress toward the envisioned summit.

Strategic Mapping (annual)	Yes	Not Yet
Strategic Flow: *Have you (re-)identified the strategic flow of strategic moves that will execute your unique value promise?*		
Winning Moves: *Have you (re-)identified which strategic moves create a sustainable competitive advantage?*		
Learning Milestones: *Have you determined the knowledge needed to make pivotal decisions or persevere in accelerating future growth (in 6 months from now)?*		

To implement an annual Strategic Design, the strategy map is best framed into 90-day quarterly plans, providing an organic rhythm and focus that integrates strategic change into daily routines and habits. This rhythm supports both the implementation of change and the assessment of progress, ensuring the strategy remains adaptable and responsive to evolving circumstances

Strategic Doing (quarterly)	Yes	Not Yet
Activities: *Have you identified the activities required to execute the strategic move?*		
Skills: *Have you identified the human skills, competencies, and relational assets required to execute each winning move?*		
Resources: *Have you identified the physical resources, information, organizational constructs, and financial resources required to execute the strategic move?*		
Expected Outcomes: Have you set clear expectations, key performance and key relationship indicators in advance to ensure consensus on acceptable outcomes and support ownership among those involved?		

Aligning your business with your personal discovery is the final step in ensuring that your leadership journey is both fulfilling and impactful. By realigning your strategies annually and conducting regular reviews, you will create a business that not only reflects your true self but also leads the future you are envisioning. The outcome is a professional life that is deeply connected to your personal growth, with a clear, future-oriented strategy that guides your business toward long-term success.

Conclusion

Leading with Authenticity into the Future

Congratulations on completing the 7 steps. Take a few more minutes to reflect on the transformative path you have traveled so far. From envisioning your future identity to aligning your business with your personal discovery, each chapter has been a step towards becoming a leader who not only anticipates the future but actively shapes it. This journey has been about more than just acquiring skills; it is about evolving into a leader who leads with authenticity, clarity, and purpose.

In embracing your future identity, expanding your perspective, and aligning your strategies, you have laid the foundation for a leadership style that is both dynamic and deeply rooted in your true self. This integrative approach is essential in today's rapidly changing world, where the ability to lead with foresight and authenticity will set you apart and ensure your long-term success.

Integrating Your Future Identity into Everyday Leadership

The core of healthy and powerful leadership lies in authenticity. Authentic leadership seamlessly integrates your evolving future personal identity with your professional life, enabling you to lead in a way that is true to who you are while serving others with genuine value.

This approach not only drives personal fulfillment but also fosters business success by creating a strong, trustworthy presence in your "metron".

As you continue to grow as a leader, it is crucial to maintain the connection between your future identity and your daily practices. By leading authentically, you ensure that your actions, decisions, and strategies are aligned with your deepest values and long-term vision. The objective here is to inspire you to keep pursuing self-awareness and alignment, so you can lead with greater impact. The key question to consider is: How can you maintain authenticity whilst evolving as a leader?

Continuing the Journey of Personal and Professional Growth

Leadership is not a destination but a continuous journey of growth. As you reflect on your progress through this book, it is important to set intentions for ongoing personal and professional development. This journey of self-discovery does not end here; it evolves as you do, adapting to new challenges and opportunities that arise.

The outcome of this reflective practice is an empowered leadership style that balances authenticity with the demands of professional responsibilities. By setting goals that align with your future vision, you create a sustainable leadership approach that evolves with you. Take time to reflect on how your leadership style has changed throughout this journey and how you can continue to grow in alignment with your future identity. The action step here is to find the intrinsic motivation to make these 7 steps—each with its own rhythm—a part of your continual learning journey, from envisioning your future identity to aligning your business strategies with your discoveries, ensuring that your leadership remains both authentic and forward-looking.

The journey you have undertaken in 'LEAD THE FUTURE' is just the beginning. By integrating your future identity into your everyday leadership, you will continue to grow in authenticity, foresight, and vision. This holistic approach to leadership will not only empower you but also inspire those around you to embrace their own potential. As you move forward, remember that the most effective leaders are those who are committed to both personal and professional growth, always leading with authenticity and a clear vision of the future.
By continuing to apply the principles you have learned, you will not only *Lead the Future*—you will shape it.

Next Step

Elevate Your Leadership

In your journey to becoming a visionary leader, understanding where to focus your growth is crucial to *Lead the Future*. The right investment and strategic interventions will accelerate your development and align your leadership with your long-term vision. This next step explores actionable steps to enhance your leadership through tailored coaching, peer-mastermind groups, and business strategies (re-)alignment workshops. By engaging with these resources, you will cultivate a future-oriented mindset, refine your leadership voice, and align your personal growth with your business objectives.

The choice of the word 'expand' in the book title, *LEAD THE FUTURE: 7 Steps to Expand Your Identity, Strategic Foresight, and Vision*, illustrates a declarative start of a dynamic and ongoing expansion. It is a learning journey, which is not a linear, one-time path but a rhythm that gains frequency and depth over time. This choice highlights the importance of continuously evolving beyond existing boundaries, embracing new possibilities, and deepening your understanding of yourself and your leadership. This ongoing expansion ensures that your leadership is intertwined with the ability to anticipate and influence future trends, empowering you to make informed decisions that drive long-term success.

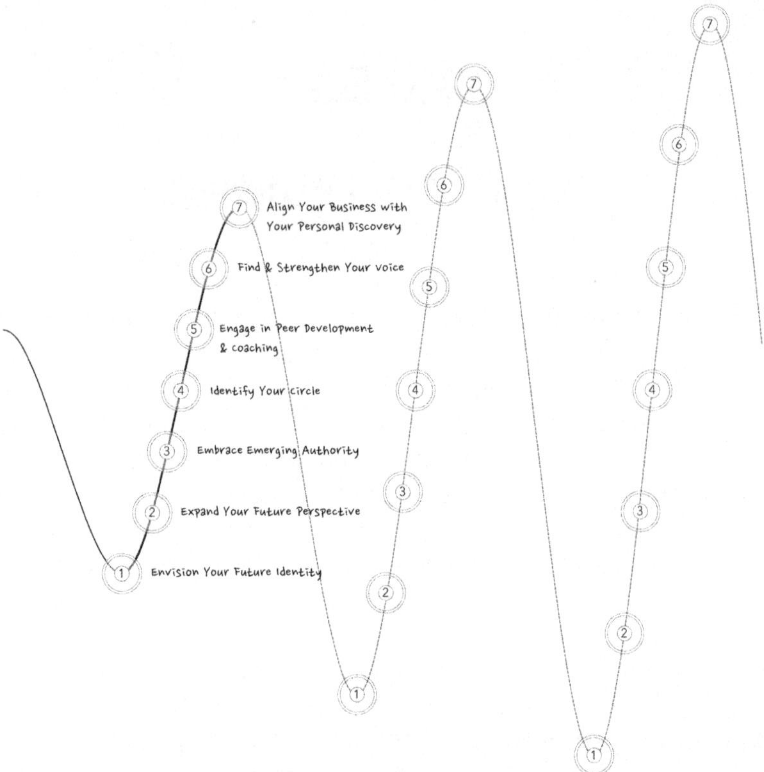

This illustration refers to the illustration at the beginning of this book It shows how the 7 steps are part of an ongoing rhythm of self-leadership development to sustain an increasing flow of influence, impact, and authority.

As you progress through this chapter, you will uncover practical strategies to expand your identity, sharpen your strategic foresight, and refine your vision, ensuring that your leadership is effective today and well-prepared for tomorrow's challenges and opportunities.

1-on-1 Coaching to Envision Your Future Perspective & Identity

To prepare and live from tomorrow, leaders must be open to coaching in order to catalyze self-discovery, empower self-leadership, and find their authentic voice. The Business Revivalists' series of 7 coaching sessions serves as a reference, offering an invitation to embark on a transformative journey that explores your future perspective and identity.

7 Coaching Sessions:

1. **Shifting Perspective:** Learn to see the present from the future, not as an extension of the past.
2. **Future Areas:** Explore your horizon to define the future areas of your life, the first step to your future perspective.
3. **Future Roles:** Identify your future roles that intersect with your future areas.
4. **Preferred Future:** Envision and define your preferred future beyond your current horizon.
5. **Future Identity:** Pursue understanding of who you can become with your future perspective in mind.
6. **Emerging Authority:** Explore your emerging authority and future audience, based on your future identity.
7. **Find Your Voice:** Learn how to become your fullest version of yourself and find your voice.

The leadership reflection is: *Can I prioritize my learning to invest in self-leadership development? Am I prepared to align my heart, mind, and purpose with a commitment to my personal growth?*

To work on your:
- Future-Oriented Mindset: Cultivate a mindset that views the present moment as a steppingstone to the future.
- Clear Future Perspective: Gain a well-defined perspective that guides my decisions and actions.
- Authentic Leadership Identity: Discover and articulate my future identity for authentic leadership.
- Emerging Authority and Influence: Identify where my influence can have the greatest impact.
- Confident Leadership Voice: Find the new language to effectively communicate my vision and authority.

Next Step:
Explore which coaching program can accelerate your journey of self-leadership development and supports your evolving future identity. Reflect on how a coaching program aligns with your leadership goals and long-term vision.

Peer-Mastermind Group to Find Your Voice, Accelerate, and Converge

Learning from others on similar paths is vital for advanced stages of leadership development. Peer learning and coaching are powerful tools for accelerating growth. Engage in a Peer-Mastermind group to explore your future identity and emerging vision. The Business Revivalists' peer-mastermind group structure serves as a reference and provides a platform for self-leadership development and refining your leadership voice.

Peer-Mastermind Structure:

- **Weekly Meetings:** Participate in 1+ hour Zoom sessions with international leaders, owners, founders, and entrepreneurs
- **Monthly Micro-Pitch:** Present a 1-minute pitch to explore new language for your future identity.
- **Bi-Monthly Coaching:** Receive 1 hour of coaching for reflection and growth.
- **Quarterly Micro-Talk:** Deliver a 15-minute talk to find and refine your emerging authority and voice.

> The leadership reflection is: *Am I taking charge of my self-leadership development? Am I open to constructive feedback and ready to surround myself with peers for growth?*

To work on your:

- Clarity and Confidence: Gain insights into my evolving future identity through peer feedback.
- Refined Communication: Develop a communication style that effectively expresses my leadership vision.
- Accelerated Growth: Experience accelerated personal and professional growth through consistent engagement and coaching.

Next Step:
Attend a peer-mastermind group meeting as a guest to experience the collaborative environment. Discover how this group can support your self-leadership development and growth.

Business Strategies Realignment Workshops

Aligning personal discoveries and self-leadership development with business objectives is key to effective leadership. Custom workshops help bridge this gap, driving both personal and organizational success.

Initiate a discussion on how annual alignment interventions can accelerate your business towards its future vision. Engage in workshops to align your personal growth with business goals.

Custom and Tailor-Made Workshops Examples:

- **3-Year Common Vision Workshop:** Develop a shared vision and purpose.
- **Annual Strategic Design Workshop Series:** Refine and align your strategic plan.
- **Future Perspective Workshop:** Define future possibilities to guide your strategy.
- **Strategy Review and Interpretation Workshop:** Assess and align current strategies with your vision.

The leadership reflection is: *What could happen if you increase your influence as a leader? Are you ready to align your personal growth with your business focus?*

To work on your:

- Aligned Business Strategies: Achieve a coherent alignment between personal and business goals.

- Enhanced Influence and Vision: Increase my ability to positively impact my team and refine my strategic foresight.

Next Step:
Find a strategic boardroom facilitator to plan strategic interventions to ensure alignment between your personal growth and business objectives.

As you move forward in your leadership journey, continual learning and strategic alignment are essential. Integrating these insights with the foundational steps from "LEAD THE FUTURE" will guide you towards becoming a transformative leader. Embrace these next steps to refine your vision, strengthen your leadership voice, and align your personal growth with your business objectives. Your commitment to ongoing development will not only shape your future but also inspire and drive those you lead. Take these actions with intention and watch as your leadership journey unfolds with clarity and impact.

The Invitation to Take the Next Steps Together

Connect with me, Arjan Visser, the author of *LEAD THE FUTURE* and co-founder of Business Revivalists, to discover how you can elevate your leadership, evolve your future identity, and refine your voice with forward-looking support.

I offer three distinct pathways to support your leadership journey:

1. **1-on-1 Coaching:**
   Continue your transformative journey with my 7-session coaching series, designed to deepen your exploration of future perspectives and identity. This personalized coaching will help you uncover and align with your emerging self, providing the clarity and guidance you need as you navigate your leadership path. Explore this opportunity and book an introductory call at www.businessrevivalists.com/coach.

2. **Peer-Mastermind Group:**
   Experience the power of peer-learning by joining one of my peer-mastermind group sessions as a guest. These sessions provide you with the opportunity to benefit from the collective wisdom of fellow leaders, refine your voice, and shape your future identity through shared insights and feedback.
   RSVP your seat at www.businessrevivalists.com/guest.

3. **Facilitated Strategic Alignment Workshops:**
   Discover how tailor-made alignment workshops can accelerate your personal growth and business strategy.

These workshops are designed to align your business or organization with your evolving future identity and expanding future perspective, setting the stage for long-term success. Book an introductory call to learn more at www.businessrevivalists.com/connect.

Together, we will explore how peer support, individualized coaching, and strategic alignment can profoundly impact your leadership journey. My role is to guide you in leading with authenticity and clarity, ensuring your personal development and business strategy are in harmony for sustained success. Embrace these next steps with intention and watch your leadership journey unfold with greater vision and impact.

About the Author

Hello, I am Arjan Visser, and I am thrilled to have you on this journey to *Lead the Future*. With over 20 years of experience in business strategy and executive leadership coaching, I have had the privilege of working closely with business leaders, governmental departments, non-profit organizations, and family-owned businesses. My role as a business strategy architect has placed me at the heart of transformative projects, where I have seen firsthand how crucial it is to align strategic foresight with authentic leadership.

For more than a decade, I have partnered with business owners and leaders, guiding them through the complexities of preparing for the future and 'living from tomorrow'. My approach is forward-looking and human-centered, blending strategic foresight, hindsight and insight with a genuine commitment to personal growth. I am not just a coach or facilitator; I see myself as a travel companion on your journey, helping you find new language and perspectives to navigate and shape the future.

In our one-on-one sessions and through the dynamic peer-mastermind groups I host, I strive to create an environment of trust and openness. My aim is to empower you to unfold your future identity and align your vision, ensuring that your leadership not only meets today's challenges but also embraces tomorrow's opportunities.

I invite you to connect with me, directly or via Linkedin, to explore how together we can elevate your leadership and drive future success. Let's embark on this transformative journey and *Lead the Future* with confidence and clarity.

https://www.linkedin.com/in/apvisser

Bonus - Worksheets

To celebrate five years of Business Revivalists' Peer-mastermind groups, I am pleased to include two of our most impactful worksheets as a gift in this book. These tools have been instrumental in guiding leaders through exploring their future identity, emerging authority and finding their voice. I hope they bring you the same growth and insights. I trust they will be well-received and serve as a meaningful addition to your transformative journey.

Scan this QR code to download both worksheets in A3 size for free.

Arjan Visser

ENTRY-LEVEL **WORKSHEET**

MICRO **PITCH**

find your future identity (unknown self)

Crafting my MICRO PITCH (step 1 to 5):

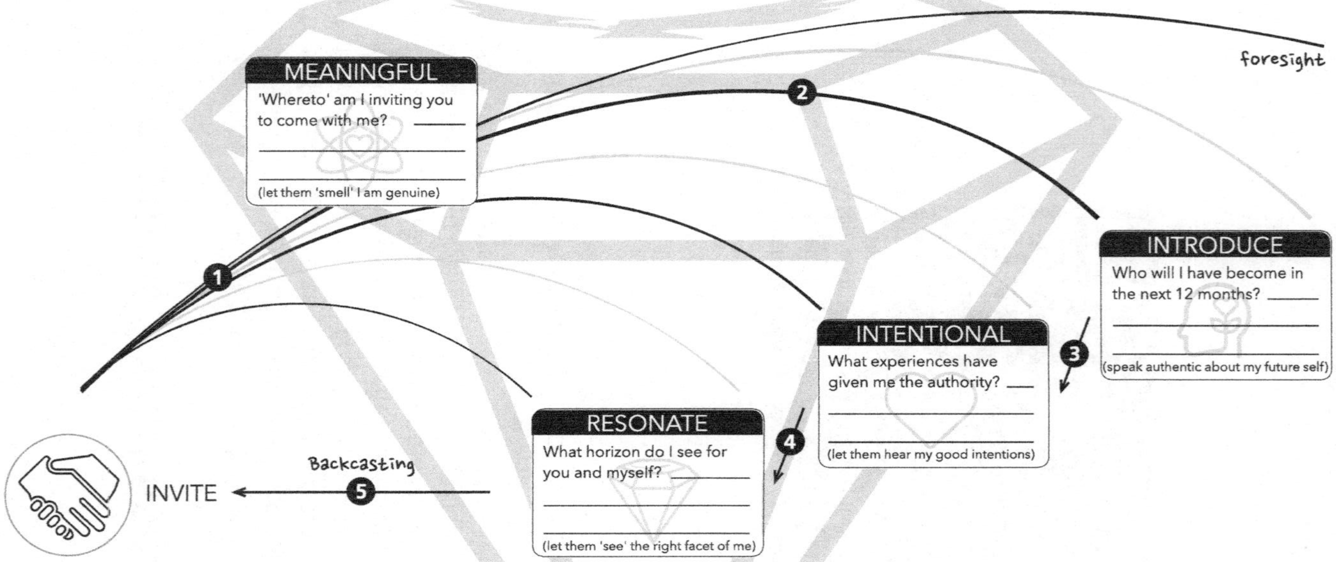

Sharing my MICRO PITCH (from left to right):

INTRODUCE
Who I am
I am a ... ______
I help / work ... with / for ...
(speak authentic about my future self)

INTENTIONAL
Be purposeful
I've experienced .. ______
My intrinsic motivation ... __
(let them 'taste' what I am about)

RESONATE
Connect with a desire
______
______
(let them 'see' the right facet of me)

MEANINGFUL
Promise my value
Journey together .. to ...
To progress even more ....
(let them 'smell' I am genuine)

INVITE
Swap contact details
Let's plan .. a coffee ...
Who .. would be interested?
(let them 'feel' I am in the lead)

MICRO TALK COACHING WORKSHEET

find your emerging authority & voice

Writing my MICRO TALK (step 1 to 5):

CONNECT

PEOPLE (4)

What story do I share to connect with the right people in the audience?

MESSAGE

PRINCIPLE 1

What have I learned and live by to nurture my promise(s)?

PRINCIPLE 2 (2)

What have I learned and live by to nuture my promise(s)?

PRINCIPLE 3

What have I learned and live by to nurture the promise(s)?

TESTIMONY

1

PROMISE 1

What 'fix' am I carrying now that becomes available when I show up?

PROMISE 2 (3)

What 'future' is created and becomes accessible when I step up?

MOVE TO ACTION

PROMPT (5)

How do I address the right people to join my journey, learn and become peers?

EMPOWER

PROVISION

What can I provide to the right people to feel and be empowered?

Sharing my MICRO TALK (from left to right):

CONNECT

Help my audience to connect with my heart, be authentic and create trust.

(vulnerability, no victim/villain)

MESSAGE

What 'mess' have I overcome and what principle(s) did I learn?

(model life, leading and learning)

TESTIMONY

What have I 'tested well' and can I promise my audience & myself?

(promises / value / to do it again)

MOVE TO ACTION

How will I exercise my authority and prompt others to engage with me?

(inspire people to take ownership)

EMPOWER

Give my audience hope. Help them to believe it is possible and accessible for them to be victorious too.

(provide, stay in the lead till the end)

7-Steps to Expand Your Identity, Strategic Foresight, and Vision

ARJAN VISSER

Notes

Printed in Great Britain
by Amazon

49692584R00050